PLATFORM PAPERS

QUARTERLY ESSAYS ON THE PERFORMING ARTS FROM CURRENCY HOUSE

||||||||||||||||||||||||||||||||||||||||||||||||||||||||||||||||||||

No. 46
February 2016

CURRENCY HOUSE

Platform Papers Partners

Platform Papers
Readers' Forum

Reader's responses to our previous essays are posted on our website. Contributions to the conversation may be emailed to info@currencyhouse.org.au.

AVAILABILITY: Platform Papers' quarterly essays on the performing arts, are published every February, May, August and November and are available through bookshops, by subscription and are on line in paper or electronic version. For details see our website at www.currencyhouse.org.au.

COMMENTARY: Currency House invites readers to send us considered responses to this or other Platform Papers in letters of between 250 and 2000 words. Submissions may be sent to info@currencyhouse.org.au. The Editor welcomes opinion and criticism in the interest of healthy debate but reserves the right to monitor where necessary.

THE DESIGNER: Decorator or Dramaturg?

||||||||||||||||||||||||||||||||||||||||||||||||||||||||||||||||||||||||||||||||

STEPHEN CURTIS

ABOUT THE AUTHOR

Stephen Curtis is one of Australia's most respected designers for the stage and for film. His theatre career spans more than three decades and embraces set and costume design for dance, drama, opera, physical theatre and musicals, including major collaborations with Australia's leading directors, choreographers, festivals and performance companies.

His stage designs include sets and costumes for *La bohème*, *The Cunning Little Vixen* and *Lulu* (Opera Australia), *The Turn of the Screw* (Huston Grand Opera), *I Am Eora* (Sydney Festival), *Pygmalion* (Queensland Theatre Company), *Henry IV* and *The Servant of Two Masters* (Bell Shakespeare Company), *The Venetian Twins* (Nimrod Theatre Company), sets for *The Secret River* and *The Government Inspector* and sets and costumes for *The Country Wife* (Sydney Theatre Company), costumes for *Cut The Sky* and *Burning Daylight* (Marrugeku), set design for *The Blue Room*, *All About My Mother* and *Tribes* (Melbourne Theatre Company), *The Alchemist* and *Scorched* (Belvoir), and *Black Diggers* (Sydney Festival/ Queensland Theatre Company) and costumes for *Der Ring Des Nibelungen* (State Opera of South Australia).

Stephen's film production design credits include the feature *Looking for Alibrandi* and Tracey Moffatt's stunningly visual Bedevil and Night Cries.

For many years he has also taught design for theatre and film at both secondary and tertiary level. He developed the new degree and post-graduate curriculum in design for the Australian Film, Television and Radio School where he held the position of Head of Design for four years. In 2014 Stephen published *Staging Ideas: Set and costume design for Theatre* as an in-depth guide to the design process for theatre-makers, students and theatre-lovers (Sydney: Currency Press 2014).

ACKNOWLEDGEMENTS

My thanks to the Australian Production Design Guild for their permission to include the Scale of Indicative Hours, taken from *The APDG Designers for Live Performance Philosophy and Practice Guidelines*.

I am very grateful to all of the designers who have shared their perspective with me over recent years, and especially the following senior designers whom I inter-viewed in preparation for this paper: Kim Carpenter, Peter Corrigan, Eamon D'Arcy, Michael Pearce, Richard Roberts and Brian Thomson. Special thanks to Neil Armfield, Rosie Boylan, Hugh Colman, Julie Lynch, Julian Meyrick, Martin Portus and Rachael Swain for their thoughtful contributions, and to Katharine Brisbane and John Senczuk for their editorial insight.

INTRODUCTION

In 1979 the situation for Australian designers was grim... A decade later little seems to have changed as regards the status of stage design in this country [...] Designers, of course, rate even lower than artists... doormat status... Disempowered [...] quasi-artists [...] mere functionaries... impotent [...] lacking confidence and prestige.[1]

Enough! Enough! This was how theatre academic and arts writer Pamela Zeplin described the standing of Australian theatre design to an international conference of performance designers in 1989. I nearly threw her paper across the room. I had begun my career as a designer after graduating from NIDA in 1979, when the situation was apparently so 'grim'. I certainly would not have stayed and built a career as a performance designer in Australia if our status had been so unpromising.

No, this Platform Paper is not a whinge about how bad things are for Australian performance designers. Our position—as costume and set designers, lighting and sound designers—is on the whole a good-news story, characterised by increasing professionalism with relatively stable and increasingly diverse employment models and a relatively secure place in the creative life of our industry. Over my more than thirty years designing for theatre I have found designers to be largely confident, articulate, effective and appreciated. We are paid (if not exactly a fair hourly rate) at least on a par with directors and actors; we are able to sustain a career as designers (providing we survive our first tenuous five or so years) and are as likely to earn prestige (if that is what you want) as anyone else in the Australian arts sector.

Australian theatre designers are lauded in Green Room, Helpmann and Toni awards, have their work presented and praised internationally, lead companies, direct and co-devise work and have feature articles written about them in the popular press. Excellent!

But there remains an element of truth in Zeplin's diatribe. In Australia performance design is only noticed when it is big or beautiful or bad. When could you say you were last aware of the design for more than its surface? Aware of the countless subtle ways in which the design supported the authorial, directorial and performative intentions? For our audience this is as it should be—the design just quietly working 'behind the scenes' to make the production work. But theatre is a visual medium and for you, the reader, whether as theatre-maker or theatre-lover, an awareness of the visual language of this medium, and an appreciation of the designer's role in orchestrating it, is a special, necessary understanding.

Through this awareness design becomes as deserving of the same depth of respect that we afford the work of other professionals like engineers or architects whose rigorous technical and intellectual discipline bolsters their public image; the same esteem of 'pure creativity' afforded artists such as dancers, painters or writers; and the courteous authority vested in a senior manager.

For the designer is all of these: artist, technician and manager. Ours is intrinsically a heterogeneous, mercurial role. My own career illustrates this: I am sometimes a set designer, sometimes a costume designer and more often designer of both sets and costumes; I work with a diversity of directors with whom my role morphs each time we work together, accommodating their needs on each production; I join creative teams where my role has merged, overlapped, replaced or been replaced by my collaborators; I create work as part of a large management team, or may be the project's sole manager; I work in and out of the mainstream, in the commercial sector but more often in the subsidised; I cross genres on a daily basis and switch aesthetic language with each new project; I design across heterogeneous theatre forms—text-based, physical theatre, music theatre, dance, each with their own particular performance demands. My practice includes other design disciplines: film production design, exhibition design, writing and design teaching. This diversity is common for designers. You can see already how, in such a diverse practice, it is not easy to define 'this is what I do'. This is how most designers like it. We love the diversity and breadth of the creative challenge. But it does make it hard for others to get their head around the designer's role. And when a role is not understood it is difficult to appreciate its potential.

Performance designers know this. An understanding of the designer's role was identified as *the* key issue requiring action and change by set and costume designers when they joined with designers for film and television in 2013 to convene a new association: the Australian Production Designers Guild (APDG). To this end designers have published a document—*The APDG Designers for Live Performance Philosophy and Practice Guidelines*—to help communicate the depth and complexity of our role, and the value of our contribution to producers, directors, or anyone interested in making better theatre.[2]

Performance designers recognise that design, ironically, has something of an image problem. In common parlance the word itself has negative connotations: 'designer furniture' is the most grossly slick, 'designer jeans' the most over-embellished, 'designer babies' unnaturally perfect and 'designer gardens' feature—*features*. Historically designers have been seen to bestow superficial rather than core value, to add (unnecessary) attributes to provide the cache of the newly desirable. Designers of all stripes talk about this perception. Applied to theatre this attitude sees the design as peripheral to the main act—window-dressing the performance rather than intrinsic to it. After all you don't really need that costume or set design, do you? Isn't that what Peter Brook was saying—just an *Empty Space*?[3] Well, actually no, Brook was very respectful of the role of the designer. He appreciated the way a production could give his intention concrete form through the design process. And most theatre practitioners I have met over my career feel as he did: directors, actors, dancers, set builders and costume makers, producers, production managers and stage managers all seem to understand and respect what the designer can bring to the production. But even these theatre insiders do not see, and therefore do not fully understand everything the designer does, because the designer's role is spread across so many aspects of theatre-making and they each see only part of it. The set builder who sees the designer in the workshop resolving a construction detail does not see them in the rehearsal room responding to a performer's needs around the use of a prop; the stage manager sees the designer at the production desk helping to heighten the atmosphere and focus of every scene through the plotting of 'lighting states' but does not see them juggling the budget to get the best value from the production dollar; the production manager sees this but does not see the hours, days, weeks of intense exploration with the director or choreographer to develop a concept for the production. The director sees most of this, but does not see the way in which the designer leads the creative vision of the production through the costume, prop and set-building process.

An overview of contemporary Australian theatre writing in newspapers, blogs, radio interviews and journals reveals how little our arts journalists see. While now the design will usually be mentioned, it is almost always in terms of aesthetics; only occasionally will it be discussed in terms of how it works, even less often in terms of how it feels, and rarely if ever in terms of how it contributes to the production's meaning.

It is exceptional for the design to be really 'seen'—to be understood for more than its decorative surface. Thematic, narrative or structural choices and issues of form and genre are understood to be choices for the writer; conceptual, interpretational, stylistic and semiotic choices are seen to be those of the director; the interpretation and development of role and character that of the performer; and the management of the creative vision of the production from page to stage that of the producer. The centrality of the designer in *all* of these aspects is barely recognised.

Much of this ignorance is, I think, relatively benign. We will go on to discover how different it is from anyone else's feeling that their work is not understood. What I find harder to accept is the indifference, or at least failure to engage of too many arts leaders and administrators towards the work of the designers they employ. Designers tell of artistic directors in major companies who are 'too busy' to attend design presentations, who rarely set foot inside the set and costume workshops where the design is being realised, or who routinely neglect mention of the design contribution in public acknowledgements. My own extreme experience of this attitude was of an artistic director who, over the three years that I worked as costume designer on the 2004 South Australian Opera *Ring Cycle,* not once initiated a conversation with me about my work. Some of this senior management lack of interest might be explained as trust in their directors to communicate with the designer: but in neglecting their own involvement with the designer and their process they turn their backs on a large part of the creative life of their company.

Designers can do more to engage with the companies that employ us too. We are up for it. Over the following pages I hope to build on this engagement, fill out the picture and deepen the understanding of the designer's role. In this endeavour I am focusing on the costume and set designer. Although many of the issues described here will be common to us all, I do not feel I can speak for my confrères the lighting and sound designers: they each deserve a Platform Paper of their own.

The title of this paper—*The Designer: Decorator or Dramaturg?*—is intended as a provocation, but also a revelation. I will dive into assaying the role of the designer in relation to two other roles at opposite ends of the spectrum. At the 'shallow end' is the disparaged decorator: someone who manipulates the look of things with a reasoned and enriching aesthetic objective. At the 'caution: deep end' the enigmatic dramaturg: someone who structures theatrical events to make meaning, and, in theatre practice today, someone who works closely with the script (whether it be textual, musical or visual) to provide a context for the production, opening up potential pathways of interpretation and providing perspective as an informed insider.[4] By marking out the territory in this way I pay tribute to the tremendous scope and range of the designer's contribution whilst also defining the particular value we bring to the production.

The performance world is seeing something of an aesthetic arm-wrestle between theatre's visual ('decorative' or aesthetic) values and its dramaturgical (meaning-making) values —between the materially visual engagement that the audience seems to want and, at the Sydney Theatre Company and Belvoir particularly, a generation of theatre-makers finding a new way of stripping theatre back to dramaturgical basics. This is not the first time we have seen this kind of tussle: romantic pictorialism was challenged by realism in Australia in the 1950s, and realism in turn was challenged by the 'new wave' in the 1970s. All just part of culture's cyclical spring-clean. Being an aesthetic matter the designer is always close to the centre of it: designer-as-decorator v. designer-as-dramaturg. Actually, the designer *can* be both, and I believe has long been so, making meaning in the production *by* exploring and exploiting the visual value of every element onstage. The emphasis may shift with each generation, but it is not decorator *or* dramaturg, but decorator *and* dramaturg: the synthesis of image, aesthetics and meaning. We will return to this theme.

Other branches of design echo this kind of wrangling of identifiers in an effort to establish their professional credentials: landscaper ⟶ landscape gardener ⟶ landscape designer ⟶ landscape architect. Terms such as these reveal the progression in all fields of design from a trade activity to a complex discipline. Today's performance designers are increasingly calling themselves scenographers as a way of shrugging off the ostensibly pejorative 'designer' and telegraphing the complexity and value of our role, just as in the past designers shrugged off the (in their mind) belittling 'decorator'. Some younger designers have borrowed the title 'production designer' from film practice to try to communicate the all-encompassing scope of the design task. If we are looking to film I have always liked the now-demoted title 'art director'—someone who literally *directs* the project with their art. Beyond the mainstream of contemporary theatre the designer may prefer to call themselves 'visual artist' or 'theatre-maker' or simply 'artist'. This play with titles reveals the development of our role from the trade tradition of scenic artist to the profoundly more complex role it is today, and also reveals the diversity and range of that role. Whatever we are called we can be sure of one thing: the designer is always there and has always been there—preparing the circumstances of the performance.

1: THE EVOLUTION OF THE DESIGNER: FROM DECORATOR TO DRAMATURG?

For some designers producing a good-looking show is their pre-eminent objective, which is great because there are directors, producers and audiences for whom this is exactly what they want. However, many of the designers I interviewed in preparation for this paper have been scornful of my use of the word 'decorator' in relation to our work: 'No! That's shallow! That's the past! In contemporary theatre practice this disdain for aesthetic, 'decorative' values, if not universally held, is deeply entrenched. But is it really any more than the disdain for the values of our predecessors? Each generation rejecting the previous? I remember with shame how as a student on a holiday job in the design office at the then Australian Opera I was directed by the company's design assistant to pack away the set models for the shows that were no longer in their repertoire. These beautiful little scale models, each in its own way a gem of carefully rendered detail in the house style of just a couple of decades earlier, did not quite fit into the boxes provided—themselves discarded timber ballot boxes from a bygone era. I can still hear the scrunch of balsa and cardboard as I did 'whatever you need to do to make them fit'.

By figuratively reopening some of those boxes, and re-examining Australian theatre design's backstory in the historical thumbnail sketch that follows, it becomes very clear that theatre design has *always* been much more than decoration—that designers then as now perform any number of complex and subtle tasks of theatrical meaning-making and dramaturgical structuring of the performance event: telling stories visually, hooking the audience and making them want to watch, showing them where to look, revealing the where, when, who and how, supporting the performer in the communication of character, motivating and shaping action, giving the production a tangible style, and most importantly communicating ideas and feelings.

Something equally important also becomes evident: that the image and the image-maker—the designer—is intrinsic to theatre. I will go further: that the aesthetic enjoyment of the image is surely a large part of theatre's pleasure and power. We diminish theatre when we undervalue its visual component. And we diminish the potential of a production when we diminish the designer's contribution.

My history of the changing role of the designer is by necessity a schematic one, touching only briefly on the many ways in which designers have naturally responded to aspects of the culture of which we are part: new scripts, new spaces, new technologies, new philosophies and new tastes. These await detailed analysis in a full account. Mine is also not a linear history; with each wave of past

Australian design practice I step forward to reflect on aspects of the way we work today.

I take up our story with two very different beginnings: in the seventeenth-century English court of James and Charles I and the founding father of professional theatre design—Inigo Jones—and in a convict hut a stone's throw from Sydney's Circular Quay in the second year of the colony.

Inigo Jones was the first identifiable designer in our English theatrical tradition, and may be regarded as our profession's founding father. Building on Italian Renaissance forebears his scenic décor and fantasy costumes for the court masques were a triumph of decorative invention that would make a contemporary casino show pale in comparison. On face value his design drawings seem to be the very essence of design-as-decoration: layer upon layer of Baroque painted visions of splendour. But if we look more closely, and read contemporary descriptions of the events—as for the masque *Salmacida Spoila*, 1640—we begin to recognise that his designs have a complex layering of purpose. He transports the viewer into another world, uses scenic reveals to provide anticipation and catharsis, focuses the audience's attention with a skillful use of symmetry and perspective, and dresses a throng of courtiers in a carefully-delineated hierarchy of characterisation—all essentially *dramaturgical* gestures. His most remarkable dramaturgical achievement is the way he uses the proscenium arch, which not only frames the false perspective illusion of the stage 'picture', but which symbolically constructs the relationship between the stage and the audience. He structures the theatrical event, literally *directing it with his designs*, so that the performers spill through the frame and join the audience—theatrically, emotionally and symbolically linking the idea of the divine order of his idealised world with the king seated in the centre of the auditorium. What Inigo Jones achieved, using spectacle as his means, was a potent, visual enactment of the complex idea of the Divine Right of Kings. For all their seemingly decorative superficiality his designs were shaped *conceptually*, by an idea, not by an aesthetic. Right from the beginning it was 'decoration' *and* dramaturgy.

If we jump forward in time to 1789 and White Australia's first documented theatrical performance, George Farquhar's comedy *The Recruiting Officer*, we find that the designer was right there too:

> *I am not ashamed to confess, that the proper distribution of three or four yards of stained paper, and a dozen farthing candles stuck around the mud walls of a convict hut, failed not to diffuse the general complacency on the countenances of sixty persons, of various descriptions, who were assembled to applaud the representation.[5]*

Captain Watkin Tench may have been describing a stripped-back poor theatre production from two centuries later; but it is clear that the work of the unidentified designer who so transformed the mud hut with paper and candlelight was a pre-eminent contributor to the audience's experience—to their 'escape' into another world and their being moved to a state of 'diffused complacency'. I can only guess what these words meant to Tench, but they convey a real sense of being transported—emotionally, even psychically. Could we want more for our audiences today? That the means were undoubtedly determined by necessity does not diminish the lesson: of the power of the visual—of the design—to provide the circumstance of a rich imaginative experience; the pure and simple power of design to move. Here we have a different beginning, and a different kind of design dramaturgy—the visual construction of a performance event *emotionally*.

In the century that followed this formative performance, Australian theatre became an established institution within the English tradition. Undistinguished melodramas, vaudeville and musical comedies performed by touring companies were typically imported or copied English productions. Theatre was managed like a business by the big commercial producers—J.C. Williamson principal among them—and their theatrical import trade was prodigious: five hundred cubic tons of scenery, properties and costumes imported from England by the largest of the commercial producers for just one year of operation.[6] In this era of pictorial presentation—descending directly from the masques of Inigo Jones—theatre design meant painted scenery, and the scenic artist fulfilled a quasi-design role as *designer-artisan*.

The standard of these scenic designer-artisans was high and their skill was highly prized. The producers bargained aggressively to secure the best of them. One such was

John Gordon, described as the 'father of scene-painting in Australia'. His skill went well beyond pictorial representation and demonstrated considerable theatrical and aesthetic judgement:

> *Mr. Gordon's art does not stop at the conception and execution of beautiful stage pictures. Even in the simplest settings he creates the necessary atmosphere—perhaps the most difficult work of the scenic artist [...] Mr. Gordon shows that he is well abreast of the times and equal to meeting the greatest demands of modern stagecraft. The oft-repeated statement that J. C. Williamson's productions are up to the highest world's standard could not be made if it were not for the services of such capable artists.*[7]

Designers nowadays rarely possess the artisan skill of the scenic artist, but our craft, our technique, is still an important aspect of our identity. Just as with any other kind of product, an enormous amount of technical skill goes into the production of a show's sets, costumes and props—where each component is crafted over draft after draft until finally the finished work is ready for an audience. To this end technical and craft skills such as researching, drafting, model-making and drawing, and the in-depth knowledge of how a production is put together, form an important part of the designer's training and practice. The art of the designer is based in this mastery of our craft—having command of our métier. But it is a mistake, and unfortunately a very common one, to think that the performance designer is only, or even principally, a craftsperson or technician. In an ArtsHub article, 'The essential skills of a great designer', designers rated skills such as creative compromise and confidence, understanding of the performer's capabilities, listening intently, risk-taking, experimentation and intuition as the most essential skills over the traditional craft skills.[8]

2: DESIGN EXPERIMENTATION

The next era of Australian theatre and design—from the 1920s to the 1950s—is fascinating: three decades and three waves of revolutionary theatre thinking brought to Australia by theatre-makers returning from abroad and post-war refugees emigrating from Eastern Europe. The first wave of change was realism, which came with Moscow Art Theatre provenance via the plays of Chekhov and Ibsen, already being enthusiastically performed here by the amateur repertory theatre movement. The next wave was the influential philosophies of designer Adolphe Appia and director/designer Edward Gordon Craig who 'called for a simplicity, suggestion, abstraction and grandeur within a three-dimensional sculptural setting that would unify the performer and the stage space'.[9] Newspaper articles debated the merits of the two opposite movements with a fire and intelligence:

> *things of the theatre must be theatrical. A set or a costume, period or modern, which could be mistaken for actuality and everyday within their own period, is bad theatre.*[10]

The third wave included the ideas of Meyerhold's circus/ Constructivist-inspired theatricalism and Piscator's and Brecht's epic theatre.

From this sensational cross-current of theatrical possibility I take one small but vital ingredient: experimentation, and one inspired Australian designer/producer of the time: Don Finley, who epitomised the spirit of the experimenting designer: seeking, testing, adapting and assimilating new ideas. On his return from Soviet Russia in the early 1930s Finley gave lantern lectures, enthusing the public about the need for the design to grow out of the text of the play, the influence of the Russian Constructivists who 'exposed to view the bare scaffolding and platforms which formed the foundation of scene building',[11] and the importance of stripping away unnecessary decoration to achieve a more poetic effect, as designers Appia and Craig were advocating—all of which we now embrace as core principles of theatre design practice.

These ideas failed to take hold in Finley's lifetime, and effectively disappeared from view until they were rediscovered fifty years later by a new generation of designers and directors. Finley reminds us (and I think we need to be reminded) of the need for new ideas to be integrated if they are to be more than fashion trends, and of the continuing need for experimentation to invigorate our art. When I look at theatre design practice today I see that we are as susceptible as ever to the habit of convention. A designer working with the Sydney Theatre Company quipped recently, 'We only do black box productions here now—or white. You can have black or white.' Why, when theatre design could be anything, does it become just one thing? The design—like the miner's canary— bears observable witness to the early signs of convention coagulating around our theatre practice.

When new ideas come, as they did for Finley, as they have over the last decade for a new generation of theatre-makers from Berlin's Schaubühne, and inspiringly for me from Wuppertaler Tanztheater with Pina Bausch's production of *Bluebeard* at Jim Sharman's 1982 Adelaide Festival—they stimulate welcome innovation and new perspectives. As a young designer I remember being blown away by Bausch's enormous white room with its floor strewn with sawdust churned by the bodies of the dancers. It made me think very differently about theatrical space and was an immediate inspiration for my design for Louis Nowra's *The Royal Show*, directed by Sharman, that same year. I remember playing around with that big room idea (and still am) looking for ways to make it my own, experimenting with how an 'Australian' big room could be distinct. Testing and experimenting in this way with new ideas is, I think, crucial if they are to be truly integrated into our theatre practice.

3: THE ARTIST-DESIGNER

The story of Australian theatre design really begins in the first half of the twentieth century with a generation of designers prominent in the 1940s and 1950s and prolific right up to the century's end. The Depression, the introduction of the talkies and a rising nationalism that was seeking expression in theatre as in other arts, broke the hegemony of the big commercial producers to make room for home-grown theatrical talent. These were the ground breakers, the *artist-designers*. They were the inheritors of Inigo Jones' legacy working within his tradition of the design as a painted picture, framed by the proscenium arch.

This is the first and last time we can truly refer to a 'generation' of designers. From this moment performance design becomes a picture of concurrent and overlapping movements. The best known of this generation were William Constable, Loudon Sainthill, Kenneth Rowell and John Truscott.[12] Many of these Australian-born designers left Australia to study and build their careers overseas, but with the establishment in 1954 of the Australian Elizabethan Theatre Trust and the prospect of an Australian theatre industry most returned; and as mature and experienced designers irrevocably established theatre design and the role of the performance designer as an integral part of Australian theatre. The theatre-going public was now able to put the title 'designer' and a visual signature to the person who fulfilled this role. A small number of these artist-designers built such high singular status they were able to set the designer at the forefront of the theatrical scene.

When we think of their designs it is those for the ballet and opera that come to mind, such as Rowell's 1960 designs for *Coppélia* for the Borovansky Ballet, later revived in the first season of the Australian Ballet. Although it is dangerous to generalise about a movement in design, or even about the work of a particular designer whose practice evolves, as Rowell's did over his career, there are unmistakable visual characteristics that could earn him the 'decorator' tag. The set and costume design for *Coppélia* is lushly pictorial in a painterly naïf storybook style with whimsical Russian towers set against a glowing golden background—presentational and boldly stylised for purely aesthetic reasons. But it is not just decoration. Taken not just on its own terms but viewed in our own sense of theatre, his design can be seen to dramaturgically focus the stage action, to define the magical world of the story, to illuminate the production and captivate the audience. In a dramaturgical leap worthy of Inigo Jones, Rowell uses a proscenium of working mechanical dolls to reinterpret and add meaning to the work and bring the action of the story out into the audience. It may now be hard to see this, but one thing is certain (for Rowell was soon to write an insightful book on design that demonstrated his appreciation of the cutting edge of international design) his *Coppélia* was not an archaic decorative extravagance but a conscious stylistic choice, an informed dramaturgical design solution tailored to the particular circumstance of that production.

Rowell described himself as a painter-designer. His generation of designers was of visual artists, trained and practised as painters, and they shared the stage at this time with artists such as Nolan, Blackman and Boyd. A fine art background, if not a fine arts practice, used to be regarded as commonplace for performance designers and many of them had parallel careers as visual or decorative artists. They were seen by the public as artists and saw themselves as such: in high style Loudon Sainthill requested the single word 'Artist' be inscribed on his elegant tombstone at Ripley, Derbyshire, when he died in 1969. This confluence between arts practice and theatre-making is now the realm of the performance artist and independent contemporary theatre-maker; in mainstream performance design practice it is now almost extinct. Today's designer is more likely to view the heritage of the visual arts as a treasure trove to be raided than a practice to which they are contributing; more likely to Photoshop than draw; more likely to adopt a neutral, de-personalised voice than stamp the production with their own visual signature. This development is connected to our present understanding of theatre as a collaborative creative act, but I think there is some danger in this rupture.

If we lose the sense of ourselves as artists we lose contact with our creative purpose and the purpose of theatre as art. Also, with theatre becoming more visual and less text-bound the visual (design) role is becoming infinitely broader, drawing in visual artists from diverse practices. As designers we need to be able to connect as equals with these other artists, engaging meaningfully around their practice, just as we hope they will engage with ours. I also believe that we run the risk of being overlooked as directors seek out different kinds of visual collaborators—outside the theatrical mindset, and perhaps more articulate in their creative objectives. As a balance to this we need to take pride in our own *particular* art—that of visually communicating a live performance to an audience—and make sure that directors appreciate its *particular value*. I was reminded of this recently on *Cut the Sky*, a powerful contemporary dance theatre project with Marrugeku Theatre Company on which I collaborated with Indian video and sound artists Desire Machine Collective. Their eloquent visual and sonic concept was fundamental to the philosophical basis of the work and inspired its conceptual development; however they were inexperienced with the requirements of theatre and so struggled with their concept's synthesis into the living, evolving production, especially in relation to the needs of the performers and the complex physical shaping of all of the elements of the mise-en-scène in the final stages — all second nature to my own practice as a theatre artist. The vibrancy of a cross-discipline collaboration such as this one is fed by the differences: in practice, conventions, visual language and histories, even in the understanding of collaboration itself, but these differences also need to be worked through to establish a mutual artistic vision, richer for being shared.

This early twentieth-century generation of artist-designers could really draw. Their design drawings were popularly exhibited, and they remain as a record of their great

23

skill as visual communicators. This interests me, because designers practising today often can't draw—it is a skill no longer regarded as essential as designers develop other (mostly digital) ways to communicate their ideas. This is part of the natural evolution of our art, but with this change I feel we are losing something valuable. With the computer as principal design tool the visual response has become tighter, less free, less expressive, even less personal and emotional. And, crucially, designers have lost, or are losing, some of the immediacy of our creative communication, needing to leave the café serviette-sketched conversation with the director and return to the computer to render the vision into some communicable form. Does this matter? I think it does. People love watching someone sketch out an idea—conjuring a vision on an empty page. It is inspiring. It is an embodiment of the way artists translate the words of a script or the notes of a score into concrete reality, literally making some *thing* out of *no* thing. But there is more to it than this conjurer's art. Theatre is so much an art of *showing by doing*, with performance as the most immediate expression of this—where the process becomes a public act of sharing. I am concerned that if too much of the designer's process happens out of the shared zone we run the risk of diminishing our creative identity.

This generation of ground-breaking theatre artists of the early twentieth century were also amateurs. There was no professional prototype for their career path and they forged their way from scratch. They began their careers working at a grass-roots level with the small drama, opera and dance companies that were starting to spring up in the 1920s and 30s. They were also amateurs in the true sense of the word—they loved their work. John Truscott enthused, 'I have a love affair with the job', and this kind of passion is evident in their work. There is an exuberant energy and creative confidence and *warmth* in their theatrical vision that we now see less often on stage (and in the arts more broadly). Of course this is partly due to the rampant romanticism that underpins their vision—an 'old-fashioned' and sentimental romanticism that is still alive and loved by certain audiences of classical opera and ballet. But I think that there is more to it. I think that part of the appeal is their command of a theatrical language—*the visual language of theatre*, I like to think—which inspires and propels the audience to give themselves over to the theatrical experience. I believe this generation was onto something that audiences still appreciate and mourn for in its absence, to do with that much maligned concept of 'spectacle'—a vision, a wonder, a visual depth, richness and pleasure; being imaginatively engaged by the visual domain. This doesn't need to have anything to do with the *spectacular*—it can be beautifully simple. Isn't this what Tench was evoking in his response to the paper and candlelit magic of the colony's first production?

We are presently witnessing an aesthetic exploration of the limits of spectacle and its absence, or, to put it another way, of the extremes of decoration versus dramaturgy. To take for example two of this year's productions, on one hand the pictorial extravagance of Gabriella Tyloseva's *Sleeping Beauty* for the Australian Ballet, and on the other the stark austerity of Ralph Myers' *Oresteia* adaptation *Elektra/Orestes* at Belvoir Street Theatre. Extremes always provide useful lessons: when is not much, not enough, and when is much more, too much? Finding the balance between whetting, feeding or indulging the audience's imagination is a task that sustains most designers and directors on every new project—asking at every turn 'how little does the production need? How much does the audience need?

4: THE STANDARD-BEARERS: THE PROFESSIONAL DESIGNER

It was up to the next wave of designers, from the 1950s through to the last decades of the last century to bring a new coherence of conception to the Australian stage. They rejected the pictorial romanticism of their forebears and pinned their colours to the mast of realism, establishing realism's stylistic hegemony for another twenty years. It was not the photographic or documentary realism of an actual slice of life but a hybrid and heightened version with every element designed as part of a unified theatrical statement. It was an aestheticized *theatreality* that evolved to offer an authentic response to the prevailing naturalistic style of play writing and performance while also—at least at its best—making room for imaginative engagement. It was a highly successful formula, simultaneously allowing the audience to look through the proscenium arch as if through a picture frame into an idealised picture *and* through the invisible fourth wall into a real world they could relate to. In retrospect it appears that these designers instinctively discovered that realism had to be remodeled to make it a good fit for theatre, and that pure realism kills theatre.

This cohort was of the *professionals*, the perfectionists who with their meticulous attention to detail set a standard of excellence in Australian theatre design. They built their reputation on detail—it was their holy grail. The integrity of their work could be measured by how meticulously the detail had been researched, considered, applied and realised. And as designer Hugh Colman affirms: 'every detail had meaning'. It was their attention to detail that produced a quality of design that confidently communicated the aspirations of an industry that was coming of age.

In the hands of these designers theatre design grew up and became a 'real' profession: the designer's role was clearly defined, their creative relationship to the director firmly established, the core craft skills of drafting plans, making models, rendering costume drawings were refined, and the management skills of supervising the design through the costume and set build became universal practice.

Supported within the secure creative environment of the newly-minted subsidised theatre company, many of these designers had additional security in their role as resident designers. John Sumner at the Union Theatre Repertory Company (to become the Melbourne Theatre Company) set the trend: using an English repertory company template he chose a group of resident designers and assembled a team of skilled production artisans from the UK and Europe who could make his productions look truly professional. In 1955 he appointed Anne Fraser as the MTC's (and Australia's) first resident designer, followed by Richard Prins, Kristian Fredrickson, and Tony

Tripp.[13] Over the following decades the Australian Opera and most subsidised theatre companies followed suit by appointing resident or semi-resident designers.

Two decades later the system was to be rejected for its stranglehold on Australian theatre-making—part of what became known as the 'sausage factory' of mainstream theatre. But in the 1950s and 60s it was a powerful mechanism for producing high-class theatre. Its support and stability fostered opportunity for designers to refine their whole-of-production vision down to the finest detail, and to control the manufacture of their design to exacting standards through the production workshops. As Kim Carpenter put it: 'Design was resourced and respected.' The design office became a central creative hub, and the designers authoritative figures within the company. Promising candidates were attached to the resident designers and undertook an informal but rigorous apprenticeship, going on to become resident designers themselves. Hugh Colman, Anna French, Sue Russell, Michael Pearce (who described the resident system glowingly, as a family), Richard Roberts and Jennie Tate were some of those who were supported into their careers in this way.

The resident designer is now the exception rather than the rule, but is occasionally perpetuated, perhaps more for reasons of economic expediency or to enable a specific director-designer relationship, than as part of the creative project that Sumner had in mind. For him the resident scheme was the perfect structure for creating a standard of excellence. In looking at MTC production photographs one cannot help being struck by how good these designers became at turning well-made plays into well-made theatre. One of these—Hugh Colman's designs for Oscar Wilde's *An Ideal Husband*—was the very first professional production I saw when it toured to my home town Wangaratta in 1973, and was my introduction to something that I instantly appreciated as a benchmark. I was intensely drawn into the production and held by the sureness of Colman's design—realised in a style as crisp as Wilde's dialogue, and with a confidence that reassured the audience that we were in good hands. The space was scaled appropriately to the performers and their actions were motivated by the careful consideration of entrances, levels and the placement of furniture. I recall (yes, the power of the image to stay with us!) how in a deft dramaturgical choice he used gauzed panels to provide the ambiguous 'post of vantage' referred to in Wilde's stage direction, playing on the idea of the public/private, seen/unseen that is at the heart of the play. Designers of this era frequently stretched the limits of realism to achieve a powerful poetic or metaphoric expressiveness, as with Kristian Fredrickson's collaboration with George Ogilvie on MTC's *War and Peace* (1966) at Russell Street Theatre. There a massive Russian icon took centre-stage, replaced by a scorched version to evoke the siege of Moscow, bringing a palpable layer of dramaturgical meaning-making to the audience's experience. Much more than decoration, this.

It is interesting to reflect on the values of the residency system today, when as freelance designers we are engaged by companies for a single production and have a more ambivalent relationship to the company—working within it but not as part of it. Some companies embrace the designer as a guest artist, give them a place to work and encourage free lines of communication within all levels of the company. I have appreciated this kind of support in large companies such as the Queensland Theatre Company and the smallest—at Griffin and Belvoir, where the philosophy of inclusion comes from the top—but too often as a free-lancer we have had to struggle for even the most basic support. One designer tells how she was savagely ridiculed by a senior administrator when she asked for a desk from which to work. We don't need to revive the resident system, but where a company can offer the kind of supportive environment residency once provided we can work at our productive best.

When I entered the profession the institution of resident designer was at its last gasp. For four years from 1981 I was extremely fortunate to experience this fading 'golden hour' with the State Theatre Company of South Australia, and especially when Jim Sharman set up his Lighthouse ensemble in which I was nurtured as part of the creative life of the company. Around this time, however, in their ongoing struggle for renewal, the state theatre companies were employing a new generation of directors who were not content to work with a resident 'hired gun' and were bringing their own freelance collaborators with them into the company. In the subtle power shift that followed the resident designers also began to look for greener pastures, and the resident system collapsed. I had already witnessed this process in Sydney, when, in 1979 I began realising my designs for *The Venetian Twins* at the Nimrod Theatre (today the Belvoir Theatre) in the workshops of the recently-collapsed Old Tote. The deserted resident infrastructure was all still there—a *Marie Celeste* design office inhabited only by the spirit of the Old Guard in the ever-so-detailed set models that lined the walls. Their brand of theatricalised realism had become a strait-jacket, hampering the audience's imaginative engagement. As a young designer I looked at them with a mixture of admiration and aversion. It was time for a change.

And change was well underway: in 1973, just a few months after seeing *An Ideal Husband* I saw Jim Sharman's *Jesus Christ Superstar*. Twice. With sets designed by Brian Thomson and costumes by Rex Cramphorn it confidently declared the new creative agenda.

5: THE DREAM, NOT THE DRAWING ROOM[14]

The designers of this next wave in the early 1970s were the iconoclasts, rejecting the realist orthodoxy and all of its values of descriptive, literal design. The three very young frontrunners were Kim Carpenter, Peter Corrigan and Brian Thomson—each very, very individual but all audaciously confident in their conception of a different kind of theatrical experience.[15] They captured the zeitgeist of the moment—being, as Thomson puts it, 'in the right place at the right time', and he and Carpenter were instantly absorbed into the mainstream—Carpenter as resident at MTC and Thomson as an associate at the Old Tote—introducing an instant generational change.

From this time theatre design in Australia embraced its potential as a tool for, as Corrigan puts it, 'expressing ideas and values, not fru fru'. In their hands the idea hit the stage assertively—as a single, strong visual statement, the visual metaphor writ LARGE: 'You've got to make a big bold statement, and then you can get on with the storytelling' declared Thomson defiantly.[16] There was no room for compulsive detail here. Their designs were defined by stripping back to essentials; raw materials were allowed to speak for themselves; unexpected elements were put together with little interest in conventional notions of beauty; and the performance space became something of an installation that exposed the workings of the production as a vital and valid dramatic component.

Carpenter's design for Rick Billinghurst's production of Stravinsky's comic opera *The Rake's Progress* at the Union Theatre in 1969 was probably the first of these ground-breaking designs with its white-box set of paint-spattered gauze and costumes freely referencing Dada and circus, and Carpenter's unmistakable playful thumbprint already apparent at the age of eighteen. The ideas of Brecht and Meyerhold had finally made it onto the Australian stage—sixty years late. As designer Bill Haycock put it (referring to Thomson, but appropriate to all three) together they 'dragged Australian stage design screaming into the twentieth century'.

This impression of revolutionary change is, of course an over-simplification. The unfolding development of any art is one of overlapping influences, and in the case of performance design some much older, established designers (such as Wendy Dixon and Desmond Digby) working at this time were also passionate about stretching the possibilities of design. However the youth and assertively modernist perspective of these three iconoclasts made a big impact. Theirs was much more than an aesthetic effect. With their directors they engaged with new scripts, theatre forms and spaces, and new theatre philosophies and practices. Corrigan talks about how influential Grotowski, especially, was on his theatre-thinking, and of his uneven success in bringing his philosophies to the Australian Performing Group. His 'poor design' manifesto, published in *Theatre Australia* magazine in

1977 includes a handwritten note from Corrigan: 'The cast [...] were not impressed. They considered that they were being manipulated.'[17] New theatre spaces were also influential. Designer Larry Eastwood's conversion of an old coachhouse in Nimrod Street, Kings Cross (now SBW Stables Theatre) into a theatre venue was one of many such adaptations in a wider movement where theatre-makers turned their backs on the proscenium arch in favour of opening the stage up to the audience with in-the-round, traverse or more commonly thrust stages where the audience were wrapped around the performance. Carpenter admits that there were many failures before they really worked out how to use such spaces, and speaking of the new Nimrod Theatre (now Belvoir) space: 'we realized ... that it is not a theatre. It is a room, shared by the audience'. New staging solutions had to be found: informal, more confrontational, with the sense of the design as part of a happening—an event of which the audience were actively part. In a very real sense the values of theatre as a playfully alive experience were being rediscovered.

Their self-confident and emphatic theatrical voices shaped many of the best productions of this era, and beyond to today. I think of this as the *auteur-designer* at work—where the designer's vision unequivocally shapes the whole production. Auteur-designer? It is not a term any designer would use. It cuts right across our conception today of the designer as collaborator. Carpenter, Corrigan and Thomson have all spoken about how important collaboration is to their work, but at the same time their work often *has* shaped the whole production in the most powerfully visual way. Thomson's iconic dodecahedron for

Jesus Christ Superstar immediately comes to mind, with its new-age symbolism dramaturgically shaping the rock opera's entire conception.

This sense of the designer as auteur is not new—designers of the past such as Kenneth Rowell and Tony Tripp could equally be thought about in this way. In my own practice I have at times worked in this way, as on a production of Howard Barker's *No End of Blame* at the State Theatre Company of South Australia (1981). My set design—intended as a dramaturgical expression of Barker's chaos of twentieth-century history—consisted of a series of massive freely-painted cloths that were removed and replaced in a series of complex fly actions (wryly dubbed 'Curtosis' by the theatre mechanists) that not only shaped the way the production worked but also how the audience understood it. The *Advertiser* theatre critic hated my set design for saying too much, but for some others it was a powerful experience. They say it still resonates for them today. This is the paradox of the auteur in theatre—and I include here the auteur-director, auteur-performer and yes even the auteur-writer who seeks to control the work through the text. The auteur method plays against the power of collaboration to synthesise the creative best of the whole team. Nevertheless, as an audience we often willingly give ourselves over to the auteur's firm hand. And we tend to remember these experiences precisely because of their clarity and single-minded power.

My reason for raising the somewhat prickly subject of the auteur designer here is simply to make the point that we do not need to be scared of them. Just as with the writer, choreographer, composer, director, or performer, if the designer's vision happens to be the most eloquent and provides the strongest spine for the production to grow around, so be it.

6: THE COLLABORATORS

During the 1970s and 1980s theatre was thriving under enlightened federal and state government patronage; state companies were reshaping their agenda under a new generation of artistic directors; arts festivals were bringing us some of the best of world theatre and theatre schools were integrating design into their training. Theatre expressed the certainty of the times. Big, complex productions with high production values conveyed an almost cavalier confidence of purpose. Design was driven conceptually, fired by an unequivocal desire to communicate to the audience the ideas of the production and its very particular interpretation. It was design as grand metaphor. With this came a renewed enthusiasm for purely theatrical values—looking for every possible visual opportunity to make each moment as expressive as possible. Exposed set changes, costumes that pushed the idea of character to *commedia* limits, playing with period and exploring the sense that 'character' exists across all time, the active manipulation of the actor-audience relationship, and a more complex exploration and understanding of the 'set' as a playground for the performers, were all consciously exploited. They shared a marked interest in the stage as a metaphorical element in itself—it was the time of post-modernism after all.

With theatre reverberating with all this change it was the next wave of designers, of which I was part—the *designer-collaborators*—that was to make collaboration the centre of our practice.[18] A new philosophy of theatre-making was becoming manifest: director Richard Wherrett described how

> *the communal was replacing the dictatorial; the democratic horizontal was subsuming the hierarchical, the authoritarian.*[19]

Collaboration became the order of the day. Some collaborations, such as my own with Neil Armfield, became enduring creative partnerships over many productions. These kinds of partnerships were not new: William Constable, for example, in the 1940s had a fertile collaboration with Eduard Borovansky and his Borovansky Ballet over almost twenty productions; and Kristian Fredrickson with George Ogilvie from the mid-1960s, then later with choreographer Graeme Murphy in the period overlapping my own career. It is almost inevitable that a creative meeting of minds will lead to such personal and long-lasting working relationships. But from this time collaboration became the central tenant of every designer's métier.

What, actually, *is* collaboration? Unless we understand the meaning of collaboration we cannot hope to understand the designer's role in how theatre is made. It defines theatre-making as an art distinct from the solo arts—the way we bring the best of multiple creative contributions together into a coherent expressive whole.

The collaborative process in theatre has a number of defining qualities. It is built on trust. It shifts constantly from the intensely personal and subjective to the more calmly strategic objective. Our roles are clear and everyone knows what they are there to do; at the same time there is a remarkable fluidity and overlap between roles where creative give and take is the order of the day. There is also a remarkable degree of responsiveness, where the process self-adjusts around the changing needs of the situation. Problems are solved cooperatively, but it is not a collective or a committee. At its best it will be led and managed, but not controlled. The director/choreographer is the undisputed creative leader but there is usually no rigid hierarchy—any one of the collaborators may direct the course of any part of the process if theirs is the clearest vision.

My own experience, affirmed by other designers, is that the nature of collaboration is not intrinsically different in or out of the mainstream. This may sound surprising—in the past it was a defining distinction, behind which was the assumption that mainstream theatre practices were always hierarchical and 'contemporary theatre' practices inherently collaborative. In the 1980s and 1990s contemporary theatre-makers rejected the prevailing 'pre-production' design model established over the previous fifty years. They scorned the process by which the design was revealed as a fait accompli to the cast on the first day of rehearsal, and looked instead for a closer integration of the visual and performative elements with the 'development model'. In those days the division between hierarchical mainstream and collaborative alternative theatre was clearer; today any kind of theatre-making in or out of the mainstream might be more or less hierarchical, more or less collaborative, depending on the people involved and how they prefer to work.

My work with dance/physical theatre company Marrugeku (*Cut The Sky, Gudirr Gudirr, Burning Daylight*) typifies the 'development' approach in which the design evolves as part of the conceiving process through workshops involving performers, writers, dramaturgs, choreographer and director, composers and others working alongside the designers. In this kind of process the design may never be formally presented as a completed conception. Rather components will be offered and trialed in draft version in the workshop rehearsals, developed through successive drafts and integrated incrementally with other visual and performance elements. The methodology is different but the objective is the same as in the pre-production model: at every step the dramaturgical function of the design is interrogated and refined to serve the meaning of the work as that meaning unfolds.

This kind of richly productive exploration was popularised in alternative theatre in the 1980s and 90s. It deepened our idea of collaboration and re-invigorated theatre as a visual medium. Sometimes this was done without a dedicated designer, the designer having been tarred with the brush of the rejected pre-production design model, as though this was the only way designers could work. To me this makes as much sense as blaming actors for the tyranny of the four-week rehearsal period which, like the pre-production design model is simply a side effect of the economies of theatre-making. The problem is simple:

the visual design components—the sets and props and costumes—require time to be realised and time to modify in response to rehearsals in a way that performance, lighting and sound components do not. So when production periods are locked into the standard four-week timetable, the design components need to be conceived early, and when extended development, rehearsal and production periods allow for it, the design can be developed later, in sync with script, performance and whole-of-project development. Designers don't prescribe the system—we adapt to get the best results from it no matter what the system is.

Whether in the alternative or mainstream sectors these more flexible and integrated processes of development take time, and in the subsidised sector are increasingly threatened by arts funding policies. In the wake of shrinking funds and rising costs every company or project tries in its own way to contain their budget by regulating the design and concept development process. The key ingredient of creative flexibility is often squeezed in the process. The price for surrendering creative flexibility is huge, as when a designer pushes or a director accepts, or when a company demands delivery of a production concept that is still not resolved. I remember the creative chaos on Opera Australia's commissioned opera *Whitsunday* (1988, with Brian Howard as composer and libretto by Louis Nowra). The music was still being written bar by bar during technical rehearsals in the theatre. A climactic moment when one of the characters was to fly across the stage became shorter by the day until finally all he had time to do was lift off and hover in embarrassed bathos.

Although these kinds of disappointments are rare, the tensions of competing needs are not. Directors typically feel the need to keep their creative options as open as possible, while the production wing wants to 'lock off' the design early to get it built in time. The designer, together with the production manager, is expected to juggle these two conflicting objectives, making our management role as designers even more important. And when the companies that employ us understand our role in this juggling act it makes a big difference.

In this context as a designer my collaborative relationship with the director or choreographer is absolutely central. My collaborative relationship with the performers is fundamental. My collaborative relationship with the rest of the creative team—the set, costume, lighting, sound and audio-visual designers—is vital; my relationship with my sometimes huge team of collaborators in the production areas of costume, set, prop, scenic art and technicians in the theatre is also crucial; as is my collaborative relationship with the managers—the production management and stage management teams. These are profound, creative relationships. For the costume and set designer the fact that we collaborate across all of these areas defines our role. Designers who are not good collaborators generally don't survive.

Because designers are involved across this whole web of collaborations we cannot be over-invested in any of them. We are able to offer a very particular perspective—an insider's outside-view—where we have one hand on the fine grain of the detail and the other on the whole big picture. This perspective can be very useful to the director, particularly in the close confines of the rehearsal process, as a sounding-board and point of reference—a kind of creative anchor.

As insider/outsiders our perspective is also of value to companies. Many companies acknowledge this in theory with structured debriefs on each production, although sadly these are more common in their lapse. The appointment of designers to theatre company boards and within the Australia Council would also provide a structure from which theatre could benefit—making the most of the designer's unique perspective.

7: THE NEXT WAVE

Without the benefit of hindsight it is not so easy to characterise the most recent wave of designers, but some of its features are clear. The role of the designer has become increasingly more professional and disciplined in contemporary theatre practice. And discipline is the operative word: directors, performers, producers and our audience can rely on their designer.

Over the last decade the role has also changed. On one hand it has become more specialised, and on the other more diverse. The development of projection as a tool has introduced the specialist audio-visual designer to the design team, and we are still working out how to integrate this role, being as it is straddled between the roles of the set designer and lighting and sound designers. The designer's role itself has become more specialised, with far less cross-industry movement between design for film and design for performance than there was in the 1980s and 90s, and the performance design role being now commonly divided between the specialised costume and set designers. This is one change about which I feel ambivalent. I miss the holist vision that the single designer gives, and it raises the bar for the director in keeping the creative vision cohesive. As a set-only designer I miss the close creative connection with the cast through costume fittings, and as a costume-only designer I miss being in the conceptual hot seat, as many directors still unaccountably do not include the costume designer in important early development. But probably the change is here to stay. The task now is to redress the bias that views set design as more important than costume design—a discriminatory attitude that is institutionalised in lower fees for longer hours and less acknowledgement for costume designers, as when in press and promotion the set design is mistakenly described as 'the design' or the set designer as 'the designer'.

There is also a complementary and opposite move, towards freeing up traditional roles. Increasingly theatre-making roles overlap and transform within and between projects: directors design, actors direct, writers act, composers author, designers artistic-direct. This is much more than role-swapping. My process on *The Secret River* in the case study below gives a hint of this kind of collaborative philosophy where designers, performers, director, writer and others openly contribute and inform each other's work with little concern about narrowly-defined roles. I think we will see much more of this, where *every* player contributes in whatever way they can to build the *whole* work. In this sense this makes today's designer, along with our professional peers, a co-deviser—a *theatre-maker*.

As designer-theatre-makers our methodology is a wonderful working example of synergistic group decision-making under complex conditions: reframing, envisaging, exploring, prototyping, questioning and learning. Ours is exactly the kind of heterodox creative problem-solving that makes us good theatre-makers. This is a skill-set that is beginning to be broadly recognised and valued in all kinds of industry. In models of new business practice it is called 'accelerated serendipity'. In the *Design for Manufacturing Competiveness* report for the Department of Industry, design is described as an 'enabling skill' that 'captures value' and provides 'clarity of purpose'.[20] And it is exactly this kind of *design thinking* that the new national arts curriculum ACARA identifies as an 'actively connective framework' for the whole curriculum. This is perhaps the designer's greatest value: our ability to responsively shape and adapt our conceptual and practical problem-solving skills to *any* aspect of the creative process as it unfolds.

There are other ways that theatre design practice is changing. In the inevitable manner of stylistic reversals the current wave of directors and designers is questioning and has rejected the assertively conceptual drive of their predecessors. This is the spirit of our age: we are more likely to ask questions than to answer them, to withhold rather than amplify our emotional engagement and more likely to play with alternate perspectives than to offer a singular vision. We can *see* this in theatre. Design is a great vehicle for actually seeing, analysing and understanding how ideas are understood and communicated, and especially how interpretations change over time. We are adept at using theatre texts for this kind of cultural analysis, but with design we have a clear window into the language of meaning.

So what do we see?

Design shows us how theatre today has swung from the poetic to the prosaic, from the imagined to the real, from the subjective to the objective. Tools like simultaneous projection, which I remember designing into a project as a student, only to be told that the technology didn't exist, are now used extensively as a directorial design tool to provide a clearly objective, metatheatrical point of view, as potently demonstrated by the director Benedict Andrews in Belvoir's 2010 production of *Measure for Measure* (although as designer Ralph Myers observed, designers are still struggling with the technology). Productions behind glass walls heighten the audience's experience as detached observers. Myers has described how he was able to offer director Simon Stone on Belvoir's 2011 *The Wild Duck* its liberating ending by enabling the imprisoned characters to step outside the glass walls of the set for the first time. On the same stage later that year Myers referenced this scenic alienation device in a second Ibsen play by giving the failed theatre visionary Konstantin in his *The Seagull* a miniature glass box as a pitiable prop, used to stage his play within the play.

Directors and designers of the last decade have once again been drawn to realism. It is a different kind of realism to that of the 1950s; it is a dystopian 'neo-realism' with purposefully expressionless factory-finished surfaces and a seemingly random selection and placement of visual elements evoking an irrational universe. The best of these productions motivate the audience to imagine and engage, but in a theatrical venture akin to the Dogme 95 film manifesto[21]—which proscribed ascetic rigour as an antidote to inflated film production values—we have also seen a number of productions so impersonal that almost any kind of script could be performed on almost any set, and with a performer's costume in one production almost indistinguishable from one in any other. In its absence these productions remind us how vital the visual is to the life of a production and to the audience's experience; we miss it when it isn't there. The potential of design—its imaginative and captivating powers to heighten, distil, conflate, contradict, allude, evoke, inspire—is, I believe, being reaffirmed.

Just as in times past, when we renounced the extremes of the too-lushly pictorial, the too-literally real and the too-brazenly metaphorical, we are now seeing a pulling back from the extremes of such austerity. This is the nature of creative experimentation—the limits can only be found by pushing them.

8: A DESIGNER AT WORK

There is no template in designing. But there is a process, and as an insight into our dramaturgical role and how designers work I would like to share part of my process as set designer on the Sydney Theatre Company's *The Secret River* (Andrew Bovell's adaptation of the Kate Grenville novel, directed by Neil Armfield with Tess Schofield as costume designer, Mark Howett as lighting designer, Iain Grandage and Steve Francis collaborating on composition and sound). Many readers will know this tragic first-contact story— between the Dharug people of the Hawkesbury River and the Anglo settlers—as it is widely known through Grenville's empathetic book and its television adaptation, and also because the production has toured widely. I give this as an example of the designer in action—as collaborator, artist, technician, manager and theatre-maker, always attempting to balance the aesthetic and dramaturgical needs of the production.

This was essentially a pre-production design process, determined by the Sydney Theatre Company's production schedule, and substantially developed before rehearsals started. An early script-development workshop with writer, director, designers and actors (not the final cast) provided a forum for early thinking. Our shared challenge was how to shape Grenville's epic work dramaturgically so that its contemporary implications would be clear in its telling. My challenge as set designer was how to 'place' the story visually in a way that evoked Grenville's poetic conception, while also making it a place the characters and the audience would want to 'own'.

Though Neil and I have collaborated many times before, the first step for me was to be cast as set designer. Directors cast their creative team in the same way they do their performers. It is a very personal choice—who will be the best fit for the production and how the creative team will work together. The designer is most often one of the director's first casting choices and one of the most important. It will not only shape the production but the manner in which it shaped.

Neil first approached me about eight months out from opening night. On a production of this size four to six months would be a fairly typical lead-in, with the obvious advantage that a longer time allows for greater incubation of ideas. For the designer's workload this means working on a number of productions simultaneously, each at different stages of creative development, and each work subtly influencing the others. A decision I make on one design influences choices on the next. In this way a designer develops their own personal style which is both a visual style and a style of working. Some designers' visual style or thumbprint is very strong and identifiable regardless of the production's form or subject—you can instantly recognise a Brian Thomson or Kim Carpenter design—while other designers' visual style is less definable. The common view that a strong visual style equals a strong design does not stand close scrutiny; a design might be strong for the way it supports the performers, the way it reinterprets an idea or solves a difficult staging problem, or for any number of reasons other than its aesthetic impact. Either way, this strong or light visual touch will be matched with the designer's personal way of working: more or less dynamic, or intuitive, or methodical. Directors are as likely to cast their designer for their way of working as for their visual aesthetic.

Neil and I began to talk and to share our first impressions of the project—the feel of the story, the kind of production it might be, and how we might work together—especially as he was to be overseas for months before the design deadline. He had similar exploratory conversations with each of his creative team as he cast them, but we were not to get together until the script-development workshop some time later. The bringing together of the creative team in this way is an important symbolic gesture—setting the collaboration on an even keel. When directors neglect this collaborative 'engagement party' it is often left to one or other of the designers to interpret the conceptual language of the production to the rest of the team. The selection of whom in the team the director brings together at this early stage varies from production to production, but the designer is usually there very near the beginning. A practical reason for this is that design realisation requires a long lead-time; but there are more important creative reasons: the design process is a key vehicle for the development of the production concept, and the set and costume designs are a brilliant means of communicating the concept as it is being developed. When people see the design they can *see* what the production is going to be.

Using research images, our personal life experiences, references to movies, art, our own and others' theatre productions, and virtually anything as a point of reference Neil, Tess Schofield and I began to make the early fragmentary drafts of the script concrete. With Neil, as with most directors, this is a circuitous process, exploring around the material to find its centre. We were looking for common threads. At this beginning-point we work like a dramaturg, playing around with the 'turgy', or arrangement of the drama, with the added advantage that every question posed will have a material, visual answer. Most of the questions the designer and director ask of each other are essentially dramaturgical: What is it we want to create? What kind of theatre do we want to make? Who are we making it for? Why? What are the source materials? How will the story be told and is the form or structure a good place to start? What are the themes or central ideas in the work? What are the central images? What are our personal connections to the work? What situations or characters in the real world relate to the project? What is the 'hook' that pulls in the audience? What changes over the course of the action? What is the mood or atmosphere? How is this generated? Who asks and who answers these questions changes from moment to moment. This is dramaturgical design, finding the best way to convey meaning visually – through the look of things. And to a lesser or greater extent every designer does it.

In contemporary design theory such questions being addressed by the director and designer are known as *wicked problems*:

a class of social system problems which are ill-formulated, where the information is confusing, where there are many clients and decision makers with conflicting values, and where the ramifications in the whole system are thoroughly confusing.[22]

The intrinsic difficulty of pinning down this kind of process is a key factor in understanding the design process and the designer's role. Even if you don't understand the theory, the word *wicked* conveys the very real sense of a lively, even dangerous, indeterminacy and unpredictability. I like the slang meaning too: excellent!

This sprawling wicked process sooner or later begins to focus on quite specific dramaturgical questions. Some prefer to call these 'problems' although I think this implies they have, like algebra, a single solution, whereas we can only strive for an effective answer. Through this dramaturgical exploration we seek out the first conceptual building blocks. Three of the many found by Neil and me for *The Secret River* were water-play, first footsteps and a plastic milk-crate. Neil conceived the space as a playground where the water-play of the Dharug and settler boys could express the potential of a joyous kind of cultural exchange. My challenge was then to find a way for the boys to muck up that would give the audience as much delight as the actors. I offered up the dramaturgical idea that the arrival of the white settler family could be like a party of gatecrashers and suggested the image of their muddy first-footprints defiling the pristine space. The plastic milk-crate became both an example of the kind of makeshift world of the settlers—used as an improvised place to sit in a way familiar to us today—and a common point of reference describing how stylistically ours would be a production in which any other thing could exist side by side with the milk-crate in our hybrid then/now world. As a working example of the production style it was a dramaturgical touch-point right up until after the show opened, when (contentiously) I realised that our hybrid style had fused into something more unified, and the plastic milk-crate was pulling focus as a too-specific aberration. (I replaced it with a vintage soft-drink bottle crate that performed the same function but a little less assertively.) Through all of this Tess, Iain, Mark and I were also swapping notes and working back and forward on specific dramaturgical challenges: the politics of representing a naked Aboriginal woman onstage, the sounds the bush would make and what would make them, and how to use light to introduce time into the space.

What I am describing is the extraordinary fluidity and generosity of the conceptual conversation. Here the director's role is crucial—the production is theirs to make and every important choice is theirs. But not every important idea is. In mainstream Australian theatre practice to a greater or lesser degree, the ideas of the production will find coherence *through* their physical expression in the design; and the production concept will evolve *through* the design process with the designer.

This is the antithesis of the so-called 'director's concept'—the idea that the director begins with a clear conceptual objective or 'vision' that is then realised by the designer and others in the creative team. This is not an easy thing to interrogate—it can sound like an attack on the director's authority; but talking about the conceptual process in these terms is in no way demeaning, in fact it demonstrates the director's extraordinary skill in collaborative decision-making—a much more sophisticated skill than landing what designer Eamon D'Arcy terms a 'helicopter' director's concept. We need to face it: the idea of the director's overarching interpretation of the work is a romanticised throwback that masks the real nature of the creative process. And it persists. In a straw poll I took as part of my preparation for this paper I asked a number of theatrically-literate people what they thought my job as a designer was. The view that the designer 'realises the director's vision' kept surfacing. The implication here is that the designer is somehow 'in service' to the director's conception, as a performer would be if they were given line readings and 'moved' by the director in rehearsal. In reality this rarely happens, with either the performer or the designer.

So how does it really work?

The director might begin with a hunch, a feeling or an idea that they would like to explore, the loose end of a conceptual thread they want to unpick. They might contribute just a few formative words to the early conversations. Sometimes they will bring one or two key visual references and early casting choices, or possibly a clear decision such as a setting of time or place. Sometimes they are very well-prepared and able to share a coherent interpretation. At others it is their first opportunity to come to grips with the challenge of how to stage the production, and to test their early thoughts. The designer may come with more, contribute more, be better prepared—or not. It is different every time. Whatever the case the designer becomes the director's informed sounding-board, knowing the script as well as the director does and having a feel for when an idea does or doesn't fit the conception. It is here, in these early conversations that key decisions will be made: which ideas will be brought forward, which themes developed, how the story will be told, what kind of experience the audience will have, what the production will feel like, what it means and how it will work. Every designer will be able to describe their own version of how the concept takes shape: how the director and designer respond symbiotically to the visual material, ideas, the interpretations and stylistic points of reference they each offer and share. At the end of the process it is usually impossible to tell which ideas were the director's and which the designer's. Director Barrie Kosky, in a lovely semantic twist, actually combines the two roles into one: 'In terms of the conceptual framework behind a piece, the role of the director/designer is very much a collaborative process for me.'[23] When the collaboration is working at its best it is a true partnership. Director Richard Wherrett called it a 'marriage', which captures the intimacy, mutuality and complexity of the relationship. When this—the real nature of the director-designer relationship—is grasped by funding bodies, company managements and producers, theatre schools and theatre critics we can be sure that one of the prime engines of our art is not left idling.

Unsurprisingly there is huge range in how assertively directors involve themselves in the conceptual and stylistic shaping of the work. Designer Richard Roberts describes two kinds of directors: the active and the passive, or as I see it the initiator and the responder. The initiator clarifies the starting points, knows when and how to make decisive choices and gives constructive guidance that moves the concept onto the next stage. The responsive director knows what they want when they see it and may actively forestall decision-making before settling on their preferred option, in which case the designer will keep the production concept developing by offering up new possibilities. Directors also vary in their visual literacy, some relying heavily on their designer to resolve how *every* physical component of the production looks and works, while others understand every element of the design in the finest detail. I remember former MTC director Simon Phillips looking closely at a scaled piece of furniture in a draft model and suggesting it should be 150mm shorter. And he was right.

No directorial process is intrinsically better, or necessarily makes better work. I work happily with all, but they require very different strategies. It is up to the designer to tune our process to the director's and to find an effective way to discover and show what the production might look like and how it might work. We do this with draft after draft of concept sketches, sketch models, costume renderings or references. On *The Secret River* I sent Neil a new batch of visuals every week or so while he was overseas. I would photograph my sketch models and draw or Photoshop new elements into the space, adjusting focus, scale, mood and the various aspects of how the design might work from one moment to the next. On this production our overall visual conception took shape quite quickly, but sometimes it takes *many* drafts to find a direction.

Although it is the director and designer's joint responsibility to meet the design deadlines, it is usually the designer who has to manage them. It becomes the designer's practical responsibility to reach conceptual resolution on time in the form of a preliminary design which is presented to the company for costing and feedback on feasibility. These preliminary designs are usually a combination of a sketch model, draft floorplan, draft costume and props designs and/or lists of those elements still being considered. They are often, even usually, over-budget. This is not surprising. I have heard some managers claim that designers do this on purpose. But every costume and set designer I know takes very seriously their responsibility to work within budget. We work hard to get the best value for the production. Each work is unique, each new production is the first time this particular design is to be realised and there are a lot of variables—difficult to quantify exactly. The director and designer continue with the process of refining their vision to make the design more coherent, expressive, efficient and economical. The designer spends many hours resolving and documenting the design in detail before delivering the completed design to the company. In the case of *The Secret River* this was about five weeks before rehearsal started.

All this takes time, time mostly spent on our own. The hours of research, of creative conversation, of trial and error, the hours spent drafting (averaging half a day per costume design, half a day making each piece of model furniture, half a day drawing it up for the props-makers) these usually happen in the designer's studio and are rarely seen by others. You would be surprised how long it takes.

The next phase of the design process brings us from delivery of the designs through to opening night. In mainstream theatre practice the designer's role switches from being an isolated artist with the intense but intermittent company of the director, to full-on total immersion in the collaborative mosh-pit. The designer is now on an almost-daily basis negotiating solutions with our co-designers and others in the creative team; with the costume, set, props and lighting production staff, the production management and stage management teams, the venue team. Observing other designers in such negotiations I have been struck by how central the designer is in this problem-solving dynamic. I would be surprised if it were otherwise: the designer is very close to the director's creative objectives and is their advocate, and we are usually across every area of the physical production. We also have a vested interest in finding the right solution. The wrong solution usually means a lot more work—a waste of everyone's time and money. Ours included. It is important to us that the right decisions are made.

Once rehearsals start our collaborative network expands even further and we become a central link between the rehearsal room and the production workshops. In managing the design we are constantly working in the territory between the big ideas and the fine detail, and often in any conversation going from one extreme to the other and back again. Beginning a typical design day on *The Secret River* at STC production facilities at the Wharf I began my supervision early in the morning with the metal construction workshop, moving along the Wharf through props workshop, scenery construction, then scenic art and the production management office, with Tess taking in the costume areas in the same way. At every step we would draw on the skills of the artisans for whom nothing seems impossible. When I reached the rehearsal room at 10am, it was to check in with stage management, and with Neil, that everything was linking in to his process in rehearsals. Throughout this production process costume and set designers respond to the contribution of the performers, the makers and the managers, and contribute in turn to the performing, the making and the managing. This process of design management continues into production week in the theatre where the designer, alongside the others in the production team, spends twelve-hour-days making the work ready for the audience.

A process as complex and variable as this can go off the rails at any time, and the designer has an important role—across so many aspects of the production—to make sure that it doesn't. Sometimes there will be friction in process or vision—the designer holding onto an idea (possibly because it is already half-built) when the production has grown beyond it, a performer's interpretation taking an unexpected direction, members of the team rubbing each other up the wrong way. On one production I arrived in the theatre for the lighting session to discover that the director had developed with the lighting designer a visual concept completely different from the one I shared with him. Solutions are negotiated (it was re-lit). Creative compromise around clear objectives is always a precious commodity.

9: DESIGN VALUE

The whole design process—from first meeting to opening night on a production of the scale of *The Secret River* would typically take a set or costume designer twelve to fourteen weeks fulltime, or a designer responsible for both costumes and sets seventeen to twenty weeks. (For the *APDG Scale of Indicative Hours*, based on the working experience of performance designers, see Appendix.) The logistics are obvious. Depending on the complexity of the production, and working at the level that directors, companies and designers themselves require, it is usually not possible for a designer to undertake more than four or five full productions a year. Do our fees reflect this? A comparison with the position in 1977, around the time I began my career, makes for sobering consideration. Designer Anne Fraser calculated that a designer would need to complete six to nine productions a year to attain the basic wage—a virtually impossible task.[24] To the discredit of our industry it is much the same today.

Designers are beginning to work more closely with companies in order to make transparent the hours and level at which we work. The APDG has formulated tools that we believe will help both designers and companies determine the setting of a fair fee for each particular circumstance, taking into account variables such as different pay structures in different companies and different levels of production complexity. Part of this strategy is intended to open up discussion on our fees, measuring the time it takes to generate a design, and the high level of creative responsibility the designer shoulders in getting the design delivered on time and within budget. We are also seeking the real engagement of employers with the significant first part of the design process before the design is delivered, so they can better support it. We would, for example, encourage and expect a company to take an interest when a set or costume designer is struggling to get the director to design meetings, or is dealing with massive script or cast changes, or when a director's indecision triples or quadruples the design time—all common and real issues for designers in the design development phase. The company should be aware of such issues outside the designer's control because they want to know, and want to be part of, the solution. Surely it is not unreasonable to think that a company could actually *nurture* the designer working creatively on the company's behalf; and support their contribution towards a more sustainable and vibrant industry?

To address these concerns, a new interconnected spirit amongst designers is now growing, in which the APDG is taking a leading role. The process of articulating what we do and our value to the production is progressing; designers have recently opened discussion with representatives of the subsidised companies on the issues that are shaping our practice today. The mood is cautiously positive.

For designers reading this paper I look forward to joining you in a vibrant public discourse about what we do, in engaging energetically with others around the issues that affect us and in continuing to make theatre an enriching and visual experience. For theatre producers, managers, funding agencies, directors and artistic directors and others reading this paper, I know I can speak for many designers: we look forward to your continuing and increasing appreciation of the breadth, depth, complexity and value of the designer's role, and opportunities for that role to reach its potential. We look for affirmation of visual values in the visual medium of theatre, and developing visual literacy through critical analysis of design as part of contemporary theatre. We encourage you to look past the surface and see what we are really doing to deepen the audience's experience.

If you would like some practical measures try these:

- provide meaningful support for the designer as a guest artist within your company;
- acknowledge the designer's long hours and high level of responsibility with fees and royalties that reflect these;
- develop design expertise by initiating Associate Designer positions in imported commercial productions;
- use Helpmann, Green Room and other awards to acknowledge Australian designers;
- seek feedback from the designers you employ;
- ensure design integrity when a design is re-staged by employing the designer to oversee the changes;
- establish employment pathways for young

designers with trainee positions within the
larger companies;

- recognise equality of status for the costume and
  set designer;
- foster the director-designer partnership within
  the creative process with new creative initiatives.

As observed by Juliana Engberg, Artistic Director of the
2014 Sydney Biennale

> *We are in interesting and volatile times. In society
> we are seeking change and yet there is no evidence
> of improvements. There is neither zeitgeist nor para-
> digm shift at the moment, so we must make what we
> can out of the multiplicity of histories and hope that
> they spark some awakening in people.*[25]

In this cultural landscape the multiple histories of theatre
design resonate. Our practice today is a synthesis of the
design legacy of our last century of Australian design.
Today and beyond, the mercurial designer brings together
all aspects of our role: as artisan and technician in command of our craft; designer as artist with the expressive
power to communicate; occasionally designer as auteur
with the vision to command; designer as accomplished
and professional image-maker who knows how to keep
a hundred balls in the air and get the show on; designer
as experimenter testing new ways of connecting with our
audience; designer as manager holding together the fine
detail and the big picture; designer as dramaturg inter-
rogating meaning, and yes, as 'decorator' orchestrating

the aesthetic values of the production; and as collaborator and 'wicked' theatre-maker. The designer is all of these. *See* what we do. We are here to help spark that awakening.

ENDNOTES

1. The OISTAT (International Organisation of Scenographers, Theatre Architects and Technicians) Conference in Sydney 1989 was the first time Australian performance designers and academics came together with international practitioners to discuss design practice. Zeplin's was one of many papers delivered at the conference: Pamela Zeplin, 'The Space Between: Political Space + Theatre Artist', in Kim Spinks (ed.), *Australian Theatre Design,* (Paddington NSW: Australian Production Designers Association, 1992): 119-124.

2. The APDG *Live Performance Philosophy and Practice Guidelines 2015/2016* is available online at http://www.apdg.org.au/ The APDG was formed in 2009, and in many ways is heir to an earlier organisation: the Designers Association in the Performing Arts (DAPA) which was formed in the mid 1970s to represent the concerns of Australian performance designers.

3. Peter Brook, *The Empty Space* (Harmondsworth UK: Penguin, 1972). The title of Brook's seminal theatrical text is often mistakenly cited, by those who presumably have not read the book, to mean great theatre doesn't need design.

4. 'Dramaturgy is the art of encoding dramatic action (by the playwright) so that it can be decoded back again into fluent events on stage (by the actors/ director)': Iain Sinclair, 'Some notes on the text', australianplays.org/some-notes-on-the-text (accessed 17 November 2015). And I would of course add all the others in the creative team, such as the designers who are also part of this process of 'decoding' the play to the audience.

5. Tim Flannery (ed.), *Watkin Tench's 1788*, (Melbourne: Text Publishing, 2012), p. 109.

6. Harold Love (ed.), *The Australian Stage: a documentary history* (Sydney: University of New South Wales Press, 1984), p. 149.

7. 'People talked about: brilliant scene painter', *The World's News* (Sydney), 7 March 1908, p.8, online at http://nla.gov.au/nla.news-article133963026 .

8. Richard Watts, 'The essential skills of a great designer: leading lighting, set and costume designers from around the country share insights into their craft', ArtsHub 13 May 2015, online at http://www.artshub.com.au/news-article/features/professional-development/richard-watts/the-essential-skills-of-a-great-designer-247661.

9. Arnold Aronson, 'Postmodern Design', in J. Collins & A. Nisbet (eds.), *Theatre and Performance Design: a Reader in Scenography* (New York: Routledge, 2010), p. 147.

10. *Sydney Morning Herald*, 23 July 1947, p.10, in a review of an exhibition of designer William Constable's designs.

11. 'Modern Theatrical Design', *Sydney Morning Herald,* 16 November 1932, p.15, online at http://nla.gov.au/nla.news-article16931155 .

12. Other artist-designers of this era include Warwick Armstrong, Desmonde Downing, Elaine Haxton, Barry Kay, Vane Lindesay, Kathleen and Florence Martin. Female designers were well represented from the earliest times.

13. Other designers working freelance or as residents in this 'professional' wave include Jennifer Carseldine, Peter Cooke, Desmond Digby, Wendy Dickson, Anna French, Allan Lees, Tom Lingwood, Fiona Reilly, James Ridewood and Yoshi Tosa.

14. The title is taken from a conversation with Peter Corrigan.

15. By definition this wave of designers was small, but the names of director-designers Rex Cramphorn and Nigel Triffitt, and designers Larry Eastwood and Vicki Feitscher, need to be included here.

16. Brian Thomson in conversation with Fenella Kernebone, ABC Radio National *By Design*, 27 February 2013, http://www.abc.net.au/radionational/programs/bydesign/the-conversation---brian-thompson/4524784.

17. Peter Corrigan, 'Carlton Designs by Peter Corrigan', *Theatre Australia*, August 1977, p.25.

18. Other 'collaborators' of this wave include Eamon D'Arcy, Peter England, Dale Ferguson, Bill Haycock, Jennifer Irwin, Shaun Gurton, Robert Kemp, Julie Lynch, Mary Moore, Dan Potra, Trina Parker, Joey Ruigrok van der Werven, Tess Schofield, Michael Scott-Mitchell, John Senczuk and Anna Tregloan.

19. Richard Wherrett, *The Floor of Heaven: my life in theatre* (Sydney: Hodder Headline, 2000), p. 46.

20. Sam Bucolo & Peter King, *Design for Manufacturing Competiveness* (Sydney: Australian Design Integration Network, 2014), accessible at http://www.uts.edu.au/about/uts-business-school/news/designing-manufacturing-firms-be-more-competitive .

21. Dogme 95 was founded in Copenhagen in 1995 by film-makers Lars von Trier and Thomas Vinterberg. Its manifesto includes a 'vow of chastity' which sought to counter 'certain tendencies' of illusion and complex technique, with the goal to 'force the truth out of my characters and settings'.

22. The first published report of Horst W. J. Rittel's concept of wicked problems was presented by C. West Churchman, 'Wicked Problems', *Management Science* 14 (1967) : B-141-2.

23. Barrie Kosky interviewed by the authors Kristen Anderson and Imogen Ross for their brilliant survey of Australian performance design, now sadly out of print: *Performance Design in Australia* (Sydney: Craftsman House, 2001), p.52.

24. Anne Fraser, 'Living on Hope', *Theatre Australia*, December 1977: 48–49.

25. Juliana Engberg in an interview with MCA Public Relations Manager Nicole Trian, http://www.mca.com.au/news/2014/03/06/imagination-and-desire-cued-biennale-sydney/ (accessed 17 Nov 2015).

APPENDIX

DESIGN PHASE	RANGE OF COMPLEXITY		
	SIMPLE	MEDIUM	COMPLEX
ENGAGEMENT	½ week	½ week	½ week
DEVELOPMENT	3 weeks	5–7 weeks	11.5 weeks
MANAGEMENT	3 ½ weeks	8.5 weeks	16 weeks
TOTAL HOURS	**7 weeks**	**12–14 weeks**	**28 weeks**

SET DESIGNERS			
DESIGN PHASE	RANGE OF COMPLEXITY		
	SIMPLE	MEDIUM	COMPLEX
ENGAGEMENT	½ week	½ week	½ weeks
DEVELOPMENT	3 weeks	6–8 weeks	20.5 weeks
MANAGEMENT	3 ½ weeks	6 weeks	7 weeks
TOTAL HOURS	**7 weeks**	**12–14 weeks**	**28 weeks**

SET & COSTUME DESIGNERS			
DESIGN PHASE	RANGE OF COMPLEXITY		
	SIMPLE	MEDIUM	COMPLEX
ENGAGEMENT	½ week	½ week	½ weeks
DEVELOPMENT	6 weeks	7–10 weeks	24 weeks
MANAGEMENT	3 ½ weeks	10 weeks	12 weeks
TOTAL HOURS	**10 weeks**	**17–20 weeks**	**36 weeks**

NOTES: A week was taken to be 37.5 hours. Hours worked intensively over the production week period have been shown as equivalent weeks.

Copyright Information

PLATFORM PAPERS
Quarterly essays from Currency House Inc.
Founding Editor: Dr John Golder
Currency House Inc. is a non-profit association and resource centre advocating the role of the performing arts in public life by research, debate and publication.

Postal address: PO Box 2270, Strawberry Hills, NSW 2012, Australia
Email: info@currencyhouse.org.au Tel: (02) 9319 4953
Website: www.currencyhouse.org.au Fax: (02) 9319 3649

ISBN 978 0 9924890 7-6
ISSN 1449-583X

Typeset in Garamond
Printed by McPherson's Printing Group
Production by XOU Creative

FORCHOMING

PP No.47, May 2016
AFTER THE CREATIVE INDUSTRIES
Justin O'Connor

In the 1990s, the 'creative industries' was a new concept aimed at mobilising the energies of culture in support of a new kind of economy: entrepreneurial, multicultural, youthful and digitally savvy. It was a compelling rebranding which quickly went global. 'Culture' moved to the top table of policy-making, and a revolution in Higher Education was proclaimed, with 'creativity' a central resource. Yet, only twenty years after Paul Keating's *Creative Nation*, the Australian Government has launched an innovation program relentlessly focused on the science disciplines. The creative industries revolution in Australian Higher Education is also nowhere to be seen. This Platform Paper charts the concept's rise and fall and argues that, while undoubtedly a victim of its own hubristic rhetoric, its rapid disappearance leaves a hole in policy-making that those in the cultural sector ignore at their peril. Justin O'Connor outlines what a new agenda for the cultural economy might look like, 'after' the Creative Industries.

AT YOUR LOCAL BOOKSHOP FROM 1 FEBRUARY
AND AS A PAPERBACK OR ON LINE
FROM OUR WEBSITE AT
WWW.CURRENCYHOUSE.ORG.AU